AMERICAN SUPERCARS

CHEVROLET • FORD • DODGE

Paul Mason

FRANKLIN WATTS

LONDON•SYDNEY

Franklin Watts
First published in Great Britain in 2017 by
The Watts Publishing Group

Executive editor: Adrian Cole
Series designer: Mayer Media
Design manager: Peter Scoulding
Picture researcher: Diana Morris

Photo acknowledgements:
Ed Aldridge/Shutterstock: 6c, 31t. Alessi:
28c. brackish_nz/Shutterstock: 22bl. Darren
Brode/Shutterstock: 8-9c, 16-17b, 28t, 32.
Chevrolet: front cover b, 7t, 9t. Robert Cicchetti/
Shutterstock: 29t. Devon: 28b. Dodge: front
cover t, 10-11c, 12-13c. Ford Motor Company:
back cover, 4c. Gretan/Shutterstock: 30cl.
Hennessey: 3c, 18-19b,19t. Jaydec/CC
Wikimedia Commons: 30br. John Machaquiero:
11t. Mosler: 29cl. Justin Muir/Falcon: 3t,
14-15c, 15t. Mustang Motorsport: 3b, 20b,
20-21c. Photography Cornwall/Shutterstock:
12b. The Revs Institute/Stanford University:
30cr. Rossion: 24, 25. Saleen: 29cr. SSC: 3b,
22cl, 22-23c. Trion: 29b. Vanderwolf Images/
Shutterstock: 16c. Vector: 30bl. VLF: 1t, 26-27c,
27b. CC Wikimedia Commons: 4t, 5t, 30t.

ISBN 978 1 4451 5145 8

Printed in China

Franklin Watts
An imprint of
Hachette Children's Group
Part of The Watts Publishing Group
Carmelite House
50 Victoria Embankment
London EC4Y 0DZ

An Hachette UK Company
www.hachette.co.uk

www.franklinwatts.co.uk

MIX
Paper from
responsible sources
FSC® C104740

FSC
www.fsc.org

Contents

Words highlighted in **bold** can be found in the glossary

The USA's long, straight roads are perfect for powerful cars with really big engines. For driving on them, American car companies build "muscle" cars that are super-fast, super-sporty and SUPER-powerful.

SUPER-MUSCLE CAR

Many people feel the Ford GT40 (main photo) was the first American supercar. It was based on a racecar, but about 30 of the cars Ford originally made were adapted for the road. Weighing just a tonne, the GT40 was extremely lightweight, but had a massive 4.7 litre **V8** engine, based on the one used in a Ford Mustang.

In 1963 Chevrolet released the Corvette Sting Ray. It had a revolutionary fibreglass body and a 6997 cc V8 engine that ran on race fuel only.

Its overall height of 101.6 cm (40 in) gave the car its name: it is a grand-touring (GT) car that is 40 in high

Main body panels made of reinforced fibreglass (the carbon fibre of the time) for lightness

JUST WHAT *IS* A SUPERCAR?

There is no definition of exactly what makes a supercar. But most of them share some of these features:

- Expensive
- Made in tiny numbers
- High-performance in every area of their design
- Very fast, and probably very light
- Tricky to drive
- Not that good for collecting kids from football practice, crossing speed humps, off-road driving, etc.

What's it like to drive?

We have never driven a car that attracted so much attention. People would stop dead in their tracks, drop their jaws, and stare open-mouthed… The driver feels completely safe at speeds upwards of 120 mph [and] it keeps on pulling long after most supercars have quit.

–1968 review of a GT40 in *Car and Driver* magazine

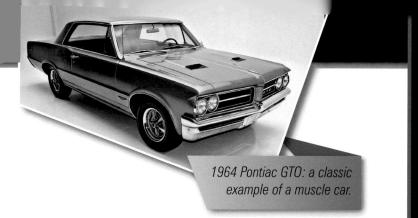

1964 Pontiac GTO: a classic example of a muscle car.

172 kph
(106 mph)

0–100 KPH
5.4 seconds (est.)

MAX POWER
250 kW
(335 **bhp**) @ 6,000 rpm

MAX **TORQUE**
456 Nm
(336 lb/ft) @ 4,500 rpm

GT40 TIMELINE

1963   1965   1966–9

Ford and Ferrari work together to produce a Ford GT racecar, but the deal falls apart and Ford decides to make a Ferrari-beater on its own

The GT40 wins four Le Mans titles in a row

Carroll Shelby (see page 21) starts to help Ford turn the new car into a race winner

Front-mid engine for balanced weight distribution

GT 40 PR

Price Tag...

Good luck! These are rare cars, and some extremely wealthy **petrolheads** dream of owning one. This means the prices are staggeringly high: in 2012, a 1968 GT40 was sold in an auction for $11 million (around £9 million).

Max RPM:
not known

Engine:
4727 cc V8

Weight:
1,080 kg

Fuel use per 100 km (est.):
17.6 litres

Gearbox:
5-speed **manual**

Drive:
rear wheels

Main body:
fibreglass (steel roof)

Frame:
steel

Braking:
steel

CHEVROLET
CAMARO ZL1

The Camaro is typical of the kind of super-powerful American car sometimes called a muscle car. In fact, Chevrolet says its 2017 Camaro ZL1 is more than a muscle car – it's 'mind over muscle'.

Factory: Lansing, Michigan, USA

ANNIVERSARY CAMARO

Fifty years after the first Camaro, Chevrolet released the ZL1: the fastest, most powerful Camaro ever made. It comes fitted with almost every racing feature Chevrolet's designers could think of. The result is that it does not need any high-performance extras added before a visit to the race track. All you have to do is drive there, then set the car's computer to 'Track' position.

Air is channelled past rear **spoiler** to provide extra **downforce** to rear tyres

Suspension uses magnets that adjust 1,000 times per second, adapting to the car's speed and power, and giving better grip

Engine management includes a 'Teen Driver Mode', which stops some of the safety features being turned off and records how the ZL1 has been driven!

What's it like to drive?

Much more than a straight-line muscle car… It's super fast, sticks to the road like it's cemented there, and is incredibly refined; it's literally a blast to drive.

– review on *caranddriver.com*

Price Tag…

When it first announced the new Camaro ZL1, Chevrolet said that prices would start at about $60,000 (around £50,000).

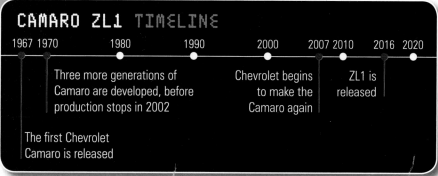

The Camaro ZL1 is also available as a convertible. The top comes down at the push of a button.

TOP SPEED

300 kph (est.)
(186 mph)

0–100 KPH

3.5 seconds (est.)

MAX POWER

485 kW
(650 hp) @ 6,000 rpm

MAX TORQUE

881 Nm
(650 lb/ft) @ 4,400 rpm

Front **splitter** channels air to provide downforce

Max RPM:
7,200 (est.)

Engine:
6200 CC **supercharged** V8

Weight:
1,750 kg (est.)

Fuel use per 100 km:
15 litres

CO2:
291 g/km

Gearbox:
10-speed automatic or
6-speed manual

Drive:
rear wheels

Main body:
steel

Frame:
steel

Braking:
steel

CAMARO ZL1 TIMELINE

1967 1970   1980   1990   2000   2007 2010   2016 2020

Three more generations of Camaro are developed, before production stops in 2002

Chevrolet begins to make the Camaro again

ZL1 is released

The first Chevrolet Camaro is released

CHEVROLET
CORVETTE Z06

The Corvette Z06 uses the same engine as the Camaro on pages 6–7. There is one big difference, though: the Corvette weighs 150 kg less than the Camaro. The same engine + less weight = quicker car!

Factory: Bowling Green, Kentucky, USA

The Z06 is a performance version of the brilliantly named Corvette Stingray, a car that is famous around the world. The Z06 is wider at the front than the Stingray, with extra aerodynamic features and a different cabin. It comes in **coupé** and convertible versions. Like the Camaro, the convertible's roof can be folded down while travelling at speeds of up to 48 kph.

In Eco mode, the V8 engine only uses 4 of its 8 cylinders unless extra power is needed

Price Tag...

The 'basic' Z06 will cost you about $80,000; the Z07 and C7.R versions are more. Adding extras can easily add $20,000 (about £16,000) to the cost of the basic car.

Lightweight carbon-fibre bonnet and aluminium body panels and frame

What's it like to drive?

Drink your Red Bull and splash some water on your face, because unless your last name is Vettel ... the Z06 is more than you can handle.

– review on *caranddriver.com*

NAME:	Larry Shinoda
LIVED:	1930–1997
FAMOUS AS:	car designer

Shinoda was the Japanese-American car designer who helped create two of America's most famous vehicles. In the early 1960s he worked on the 1963 Corvette Stingray, one of the most beautiful cars of the time. Then in the late 1960s and early 1970s he was the main designer for the Ford Mustang (see page 30).

Another version of the Z06 – the Z07 – has extra carbon-fibre parts for lightness, improved brakes and different aerodynamics, and produces the most downforce of any street car Chevrolet has ever made.

Onboard computers can be set to five different driving modes: Weather, Eco, Tour, Sport and Track

Vents behind front wheels channel heat away from the brakes

TOP SPEED

298 kph (est.)
(211 mph)

0–100 KPH

2.9 seconds*

MAX POWER

485 kW
(650 bhp) @ 6,400 rpm

MAX TORQUE

881 Nm
(650 lb/ft) @ 3,600 rpm

 Max RPM:
7,200

Engine:
6200 cc supercharged V8

 Weight:
1,600 kg

 Fuel use per 100 km:
17.7 litres*

CO2:
322 g/km*

 Gearbox:
6-speed manual or 8-speed automatic

Drive:
rear wheels

 Main body:
aluminium

Frame:
aluminium

Braking:
carbon-ceramic
*figures for automatic gearbox

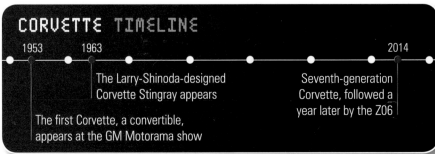

CORVETTE TIMELINE

1953   1963   2014

The Larry-Shinoda-designed Corvette Stingray appears

The first Corvette, a convertible, appears at the GM Motorama show

Seventh-generation Corvette, followed a year later by the Z06

Is the Hellcat the most muscular American muscle car ever built? Some people think so. Try this fact for size – in 2015, when the Hellcat was released, the most powerful **production cars** in the world were:

[
1 Ferrari F12
2 Dodge Challenger SRT Hellcat
3 Lamborghini Aventador
]

Factory: Brampton, Ontario, Canada

RETRO
The Hellcat's design has reminders of the 1970 Dodge **HEMI** Challenger, including the double headlights and sidelines that rise under the rear window. The modern Hellcat comes with two different keys:

THE BLACK KEY
Turns the Hellcat into a pussycat by restricting the power and speed of the car in several ways, including stopping a lot of the engine's power and limiting the rpm.

THE RED KEY
This is MUCH more fun. The full-power engine, ear-splitting exhaust and launch control system are all available. With the red key in the ignition, the Hellcat really starts to spit!

SRT HELLCAT TIMELINE

1958   1970   2008

The modern Challenger comes out. In 2015 the super-powerful SRT version appears.

A new Challenger, much more of a muscle car than the first, is released

The first Challenger appears. These first cars were powerful, but more like family cars than supercars.

A Dodge HEMI Challenger from 1970: a lot slower than a Hellcat, but still visibly its grandad.

TOP SPEED
328 kph

0–100 KPH
3.5 seconds

MAX POWER
527 kW
(707 bhp) @ 6,100 rpm

MAX TORQUE
881 Nm
(650 lb/ft) @ 4,200 rpm

Paddle shifters behind the steering wheel let the driver change gear without taking a hand off the wheel

Automatic 8-speed gearbox specially designed to handle the power of the engine

Air intake in the bonnet feeds air to the engine's supercharger

Where the inside-left headlight should be is an air intake for the engine

Max RPM:
not known

Engine:
6200 cc supercharged HEMI V8

Weight:
1,925 kg

Fuel use per 100 km:
16.6 litres

CO2:
not known

Gearbox:
8-speed automatic or 6-speed manual

Drive:
rear wheels

Main body:
steel/aluminium

Frame:
steel

Braking:
steel

What's it like to drive?

It's a kind of fun that's always tinged with a bit of fear. You'll laugh out loud during hard acceleration on a big empty road, but it will be a nervous laugh, and when you're done you'll wipe your sweaty palms on your jeans.

– review on *jalopnik.com*

DODGE
VIPER ACR

ACR stands for American Club Racer, which tells you most of what you need to know about this car. It is designed for going around a racetrack – very quickly.

Factory: Detroit, Michigan, USA

The Viper ACR is a high-performance version of the Dodge Viper. Surprisingly it actually has a lower top speed than the Viper: 285 kph versus 300 kph plus for the basic car, but the ACR has aerodynamic features that a) slow it down and b) increase downforce.

Enormous 8.4 litre engine is front-mid mounted

Carbon-fibre bonnet: central air intake feeds air to the engine, side vents help with cooling

Huge front splitter channels air to provide downforce for front tyres

The monster engine is constructed entirely from aluminium.

Price Tag...

Hurry, if you want a new one: in 2016 Dodge announced that it would stop making the Viper in 2017. The starting price is $118,795 (£96,000) – but that's just the start. Adding racing stripes (and you would need those) costs $5,000 (£4,000). A bit of extra carbon fibre outside is another $5,100 (£4,100), and improving the aerodynamics even more costs $6,900 (£5,600).

VIPER ACR TIMELINE

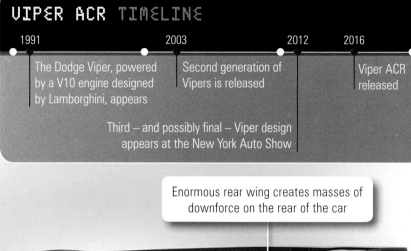

1991	2003	2012	2016

The Dodge Viper, powered by a V10 engine designed by Lamborghini, appears

Second generation of Vipers is released

Viper ACR released

Third – and possibly final – Viper design appears at the New York Auto Show

Enormous rear wing creates masses of downforce on the rear of the car

Racecar-inspired side exhaust vents

ACR EXTREME
The most full-on version of the ACR is the ACR Extreme. It has the same power as the 'normal' ACR, but an even bigger front splitter and wing. At high speed the Extreme's aerodynamics create over 900 kg of downforce. That's the equivalent of six giant pandas sitting on the roof.

What's it like to drive?

This is the ultimate pursuit vehicle. Every [police force] should have one, as it will out-manoeuvre any other car on the road today. Criminals would ... surrender at the mere sight of it in their rearview mirror.

– former *Top Gear* presenter Chris Evans reviews the Viper ACR

TOP SPEED
285 kph

0–100 KPH
3.5 seconds

MAX POWER
481 kW
(645 bhp) @ 6,150 rpm

MAX TORQUE
813 Nm
(600 lb/ft) @ 4,950 rpm

 Max RPM:
7,000

 Engine:
8382 cc V10

 Weight:
1,520 kg

 Fuel use per 100 km:
15.2 litres

 CO2:
380 g/km

 Gearbox:
6-speed manual

 Drive:
rear wheels

 Main body:
aluminium/carbon fibre

 Frame:
magnesium/ aluminium/steel

 Braking:
carbon-ceramic

FALCON
F7

The F7 is an American supercar most European petrolheads haven't even heard of. It's their loss: the F7 is filled with features that will be familiar to fans of British, Italian or German supercars:

- The car is super lightweight, with lots of carbon fibre
- It is brimming with technology and advanced materials
- It has a carbon interior and race-car manual gearbox.

The F7 shares one feature with its muscle car buddies, though: massive power. The standard car produces about 460 kW, but the twin-turbo version of the engine generates more than double that. In fact, with 821 kW it creates more power than a Porsche 918 Spyder or Zonda Revolucion!

Factory: Detroit, Michigan, USA

The most extreme F7 is powered by a twin-turbo V8 engine

Front and side aerodynamic features add downforce

Huge air intake at the front sucks air under the car

What's it like to drive?

The best part about going fast in the Falcon F7 is the sound of its V8. It's much louder than its Corvette counterpart!

– review on *edmunds.com*

Price Tag...

It's hard to be exact about how much it will cost, because each car is hand built for each buyer. The 'basic' F7 with a 460 kW engine costs about $295,000 (£250,000), and the twin-turbo 820 kW engine version is about $395,000 (£320,000).

TOP SPEED
320+ kph
(202 mph)

0–100 KPH
2.8 seconds

MAX POWER
821 kW
(1,100 bhp) @ 6,600 rpm

MAX TORQUE
793 Nm
(585 lb/ft) @ 5,400 rpm (standard engine)

Many parts of the F7's design were inspired by jet fighters, including the instrument gauges on the dashboard.

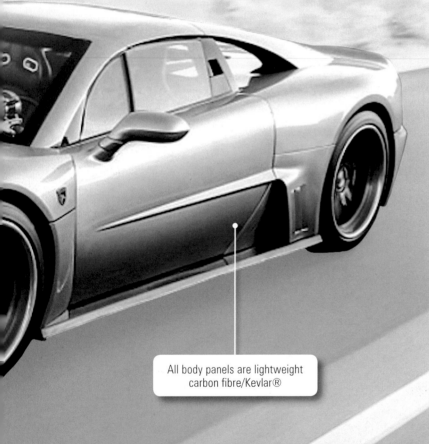

All body panels are lightweight carbon fibre/Kevlar®

Max RPM:
7,200 (est.)

Engine:
6200 cc

Weight:
1,265 kg

Fuel use per 100 km:
not known

CO2:
not known

Gearbox:
6-speed manual

Drive:
rear wheels

Main body:
carbon fibre/**Kevlar**®

Frame:
aluminium/carbon fibre/Kevlar®

Braking:
carbon-ceramic

F7 TIMELINE

2009   2011   2012

The first F7 is sold

A prototype F7 appears at the Detroit Motor Show

Jeff Lemke decides he'd like to design and build a supercar in North America

FORD
GT

In 1966, Ford's GT40 famously beat Ferrari at the Le Mans 24-hour endurance race. Sixty years later, a new GT also crossed the Le Mans finish line in first.* A minute behind in second place was a Ferrari 488 GTE.

DESIGN AIMS

In 2016, Ford's engineers were asked what had been the most important considerations when designing the GT. They replied, "Lap times, lap times and lap times." So, this car is designed to go fast around a racetrack, but it can also be driven on the road.

The exhaust leaves the GT in the middle of the car's rear – like on the 1966 GT40.

Lightweight windscreen made of the same material as smartphone screens

Front grille channels air over bonnet, adding front downforce

Price Tag...

For 2017, Ford made 500 GTs for specially chosen customers. The chosen few paid a price estimated to be $450,000 +.

Ride height can be adjusted by up to 50 mm

*GTs were also third, fourth and ninth.

GT TIMELINE

1966 ● ● ● ● ● **2005** ● **2016** ● ●

Ford GT40 wins the Le Mans
endurance race the first of four times

Ford releases a GT model (development project
codename: 'Petunia'), which it sells 2005–06

All-new GT wins at Le Mans; road-car version is
scheduled for release in late 2016

TOP SPEED

320+** kph
(200+ mph)

0–100 KPH

3.3** seconds

MAX POWER

450+** kW
(603 bhp)

MAX TORQUE

800 Nm
(590 lb/ft)

What's it like **NOT** to drive one?

*Thank you for your interest in purchasing a Ford GT... We
are thrilled that you share our passion for performance
and the all-new Ford GT. Unfortunately, we do not have
enough Ford GTs to fulfil your request at this time.*

– extract from the letter sent to the 6,500+ people
who wanted to buy a GT but weren't allowed to

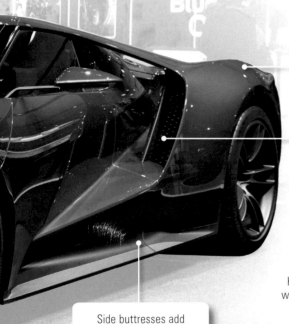

Rear spoiler can be raised
or lowered and can even
be used as an air brake

Side buttresses add
downforce to the rear tyres

Huge air intakes in front of rear
wheels feed cooling air to brakes,
and channel air to engine

OWNING A GT

Over 7,000 people wanted to
buy a GT, but the company only
made 500. You had to earn the
right to buy one. Ford put out a
long questionnaire asking which
other Fords you had owned, and
whether you were planning to
actually drive the car (or just put it
in a warehouse).

**estimated figures

Max RPM:
not known

Engine:
3500 cc twin-turbo V6

Weight:
1,400** kg

Fuel use per 100 km:
not known

CO2:
not known

Gearbox:
7-speed dual-clutch
automatic

Drive:
rear wheels

Main body:
carbon fibre

Frame:
aluminium/carbon fibre

Braking:
carbon-ceramic

HENNESSEY
VENOM GT

In 2013, the Venom GT became the quickest production car to 300 kph (it took just 13 seconds). Two months later it reached a top speed of 435.3115 kph. Even for a supercar, this is REALLY fast!

The Venom GT came to exist after another Venom, the Viper, had beaten a Bugatti Veyron to become the fastest car to 321.87 kph (200 mph). John Hennessey, who owns the Venom company, said,

"I joked about putting the Viper engine in the back of a Lotus Exige." The Exige is one of the lightest supercars around: putting the world's quickest engine in the back of it was a crazy idea.

"Then I thought, let's do a sketch and see what that might look like. When I saw the sketch I stopped laughing."

What's it like to drive?

I wake up in the middle of the night thinking about the speed. What it would be like to take something like this to the 24 Hours of Nürburgring? It's just so fast.

– review from *Jalopnik/wired.com*

Price Tag...

If you need to ask, you can't afford it: the Venom GT costs $1.2 million (almost £1 million). And that's before you dip into the optional extras list — which includes what must be the best optional extra ever: 'Stereo System Designed by Stephen Tyler of Aerosmith'.

7.0 litre V8 engine generates 1 bhp per kg of weight

Side vents in front of rear wheels channel air into the engine bay

Side vents behind front wheels release air, helping move heat away from the front brakes

The original design sketches, imagining what a lightweight Lotus with the world's fastest engine in the back might look like.

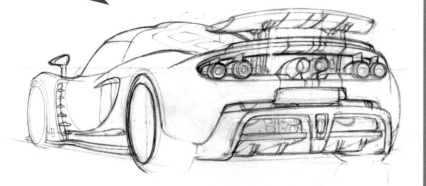

TOP SPEED

435.3115 kph
(270.49002575 mph)

0–100 KPH

2.8 seconds

MAX POWER

928 kW
(1,244 bhp) @ 6,600 rpm

MAX TORQUE

1566 Nm
(1,155 lb/ft) @ 4,400 rpm

VENOM GT TIMELINE

2007 2011 2013

A Venom Viper beats a Bugatti Veyron to become the fastest car to reach 200 mph (321 kph); the idea for the GT version is born

The Venom GT goes on sale

The Venom GT becomes the fastest car to reach 300 kph

Air is channelled through front grille, up on to bonnet and over roof, improving downforce

 Max RPM:
7,200

 Engine:
7000 cc twin-turbo V8

 Weight:
1,244 kg

 Fuel use per 100 km:
14.8 litres

 CO2:
334 g/km

 Gearbox:
6-speed manual

 Drive:
rear wheels

 Main body:
carbon fibre

 Frame:
carbon fibre/aluminium

 Braking:
carbon-ceramic

SHELBY
SUPER SNAKE (2015)

Factory: Las Vegas, Nevada, USA

"The Shelby Super Snake", says the brochure, "is the supercharged muscle car by which all others are measured…". This is fighting talk – but then, the Super Snake IS as powerful as a Lamborghini Aventador.

MUSTANG TO SUPER SNAKE

Every Super Snake starts life as a Ford Mustang muscle car – then it has a bit more muscle added. The 'basic' version of the Super Snake is then fitted with a Ford Performance V8 engine with a supercharger. This produces 485 kW of power, which is more than an Aston Martin V12 Zagato. Some customers, though, want even more power. For them there's a version of the engine that produces over 600+ kW of power.

Carbon-fibre bonnet, front splitter, rear spoiler and other parts make the car lighter

New wheels and more powerful brakes than a normal Mustang

The front of the Super Snake is lowered and fitted with new aerodynamic parts, including a carbon front splitter.

Price Tag…

First you have to buy a Ford Mustang. Then you give it to Shelby, plus about $50,000 (around £40,000) – a bit more than that if you want the 600+ kW version. A little while later, Shelby gives you back a Super Snake. (It gets to keep the bits it took off your Mustang.)

SUPER SNAKE TIMELINE

1967 · · · · · **2007** **2015**

Shelby designs the first Super Snake, capable of 254 kph, but does not go ahead with production because costs are too high

The firm offers a Super Snake conversion of the Ford GT500

The current Super Snake appears

Different gearing for fast acceleration, and a new, faster-shifting gear mechanism in the cabin

Exhaust improves engine's function by removing waste gases more efficiently

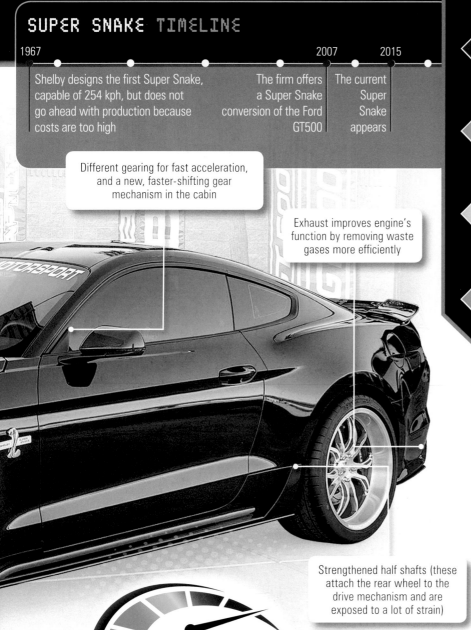

Strengthened half shafts (these attach the rear wheel to the drive mechanism and are exposed to a lot of strain)

What's it like to drive?

This Super Snake is too much of everything...
This is the biggest, baddest Mustang that Shelby
makes, aimed at drivers who want people to
notice them. Is it a true Shelby? Absolutely.

– review on *roadandtrack.com*

NAME:	Carroll Shelby
LIVED:	1923–2012
FAMOUS AS:	racing driver and car designer

After racing in Formula 1 and winning the Le Mans endurance race in 1959, Shelby started Shelby-American. His company is famous for **tuning** performance cars to give them more power. Shelby is especially famous for his work on Dodge and Ford cars.

TOP SPEED
322 kph
(200 mph)

0–100 KPH
4.0 seconds

MAX POWER
634 kW
(850 bhp) @ 7,400 rpm

MAX TORQUE
868 Nm
(640 lb/ft) @ 6,400 rpm

 Max RPM:
7,400

 Engine:
4951 cc
supercharged V8

 Weight:
1,738 kg

 Fuel use per 100 km:
not known

 CO2:
not known

 Gearbox:
6-speed manual

 Drive:
rear wheels

 Main body:
steel, aluminium, carbon fibre

 Frame:
steel/aluminium

 Braking:
steel

SSC
TUATARA

The Tuatara is SSC's newest model, and it has a lot to live up to. It is the replacement for the company's Ultimate Aero – which from 2007 to 2010 was the world's fastest production car.

Factory: West Richland, Washington State, USA

CHALLENGING THE VEYRON SUPER SPORT

The Tuatara has been designed to challenge the car that took the World's Fastest Production Car crown from the Ultimate Aero: the Bugatti Veyron Super Sport. The Super Sport can do 431.072 kph (though it is usually **limited** to 415 kph, because above that speed the tyres might disintegrate!).

Very low roof height of only just over 1 m

Low nose section, very close to the ground

WHAT'S WITH THE NAME?

A tuatara is a lizard-like animal from New Zealand. It is said that the tuatara lizard can adapt and develop more quickly than any other animal. Which makes it a great name for a supercar.

Futuristic bubble covers driver and passenger

Price Tag...

SSC says the price of the Tuatara will be $1.3 million (just over £1 million) when production models are available for sale.

What's it like to drive?

*I've never personally seen **exhaust headers** glow orange/red for that long period of time. I was waiting for metal to start dripping on the floor.*

– Jerod Shelby, the Tuatara's designer, describes putting the Tuatara through extreme testing

Air flows through side struts and either into engine bay or towards aerodynamic features at rear of car

Rear wings copied from the aircraft industry help stabilise the car and add grip

Floor designed to cause air to flow faster underneath the car than above it – this 'Venturi effect' adds downforce

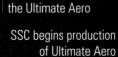

TUATARA TIMELINE

Early 2000s	2006	2007	2011	2017
SSC start to develop the Ultimate Aero		Ultimate Aero becomes the world's fastest production car	Development of the Tuatara begins	The first production Tuataras are scheduled for delivery
SSC begins production of Ultimate Aero				

TOP SPEED

444 kph
(276 mph)

0–100 KPH

2.5 seconds

MAX POWER

1007 kW
(1,350 bhp) @ 6,800 rpm

MAX TORQUE

1413 Nm
(1,042 lb/ft) @ 6,800 rpm

Max RPM:
9,200

Engine:
6942 cc twin-turbo V8

Weight:
1,247 kg

Fuel use per 100 km:
not known

CO2:
not known

Gearbox:
7-speed manual

Drive:
rear wheels

Main body:
carbon fibre

Frame:
carbon fibre/aluminium

Braking:
carbon-ceramic

ROSSION

Q1

Rossion makes two versions of this car. The 'normal' Q1 is designed for use on roads and the Q1R is a track-performance car. The Q1R has 10 per cent more power.

Both Q1 designs are based on the Noble M400, a snarling, raw supercar that used to be made in Britain. Rossion bought the design in 2007, and started making improvements that would make the car more luxurious. The Q1 has the same windscreen as the M400, but just about everything else on the outside is changed. The inside design, suspension and engine are all different too.

Factory: Palm Beach County, Florida, USA

HANS safety harness, for additional driver safety

Inside, leather-coated carbon-fibre seats are comfortable yet lightweight

Rear spoiler and diffuser add grip to rear tyres at high speeds

Rear vents channel air towards aerodynamic features at back of car

Front splitter channels air up over bonnet and under car

RACE READY Q1R

The race version of the Q1 is changed even further from the original M400 design. It is supplied with a reinforced frame and fire-extinguishing systems for the cabin and engine bay.

All kinds of adjustments to the suspension can be made, to set the car up for different tracks. And the Q1R comes fitted with a massive rear spoiler, to add extra downforce.

Q1 TIMELINE

2007 — The first Q1s are sold as **kit cars**, which owners can build themselves

2013 — The Q1R is introduced

2008 — Rossion buys the rights to the Noble M400 design

The Q1R, the race-ready version of the Rossion supercar.

TOP SPEED
304 kph
(189 mph)

0–100 KPH
3.3 seconds

MAX POWER
336 kW
(450 bhp) @ 5,800 rpm

MAX TORQUE
529 Nm
(390 lb/ft) @ 4,400 rpm

What's it like to drive?

The driving position is like being inside a machine-gun pillbox ... the turbocharged Ford V6 settles into a rumbling idle with the occasional popping and burbling [and] we can tell you that this car is brutally fast.

– review on *autoguide.com*

Price Tag...

Having a Q1 built will cost you at least $100,000 – more if you dip into the extras catalogue for things like racing stripes, painted wheels or a carbon-fibre splitter or rear spoiler.

Max RPM:
7,000

Engine:
2999 cc twin-turbo V6

Weight:
1,043 kg

Fuel use per 100 km:
15.1 litres

CO2:
not known

Gearbox:
6-speed manual

Drive:
rear wheels

Main body:
carbon-Kevlar®

Frame:
steel

Braking:
steel

VLF
FORCE 1 V10

How many supercars can reach 100 kph in just over 3 seconds, but come fitted with a holder between the seats for two bottles of champagne? Just one! And the VLF Force 1 V10 is it.

Factory: Auburn Hills, Michigan, USA

The Force 1 is very loosely based on another aggressive-looking car, the Dodge Viper (see page 12). The **chassis** is based on a Viper's, and like the Viper the Force 1 is powered by an 8.4 litre V10 engine … but this particular V10 is 75 kW more powerful than the Viper's. Just about everything else about the car is completely different. It has a new carbon-fibre body shape, new seats and interior, and different brakes and wheels.

Small roof spoiler improves aerodynamics, and contains a high-level brake light and the car's onboard WiFi system

Computer-controlled suspension makes adjustments up to 10,000 times per second, improving comfort and grip

Wheels are a **concave** design that allows less alloy to be used for the same strength

NAME:	Henrik Fisker
LIVED:	1963–present
FAMOUS AS:	car designer

Fisker is the 'F' in VLF. He was born in Denmark, where (like many boys) he loved sketching car designs. Fisker kept sketching, though, and today he is one of the world's leading car designers. He worked on the designs for the BMW Z8; the Aston Martin DB9 and V8 Vantage; the Fisker Karma luxury petrol-electric sports car; and the Force 1.

Price Tag…

Prices start at $268,500 (around £220,000). This is a lot of money – as much as a Lamborghini Huracán – but in 2016 VLF said it only initially planned to make 50 Force 1s. Not only is this a fast supercar, but it is also rare.

FORCE 1 V10 TIMELINE

2012 — VLF unveils its first car, the Destino, a V8-engined car based on designer Henrik Fisker's petrol-electric Karma

2015 — Work starts on the Force 1 V10

2016 — Finished Force 1 V10 appears at the Detroit Auto Show; the first vehicles are scheduled for delivery in late 2016

What's it like to drive?

"A hypercar-worrying top speed... and a 0-60 mph time of three seconds flat. That naturally aspirated V10 feeds the rear wheels through a six-speed manual gearbox, with a six-speed automatic optional. Considering the performance, its starting price of $268,000 almost seems like a bargain."

– review on *autoexpress.co.uk*

V10 engine – one of the most powerful non-turbo engines in the world

*The Fisker Karma, a petrol-electric **hybrid** sports car designed by Henrik Fisker. Karmas are said to have been owned by the singer Justin Bieber, former US Vice President Al Gore, actor Leonardo DiCaprio, and former US Secretary of State General Colin Powell.*

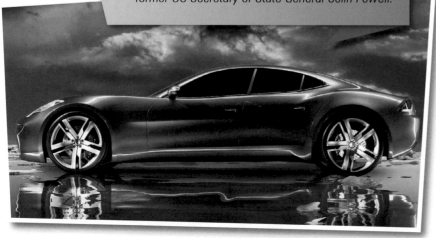

TOP SPEED (est.)
351 kph
(268 mph) (limited)

0–100 KPH
3.1 seconds

MAX POWER
556 kW
(745 bhp) @ 6,100 rpm

MAX TORQUE
865 Nm
(638 lb/ft) @ 5,000 rpm

Max RPM:
not known

Engine:
8400 cc V10

Weight:
1,538 kg

Fuel use per 100 km:
not known

CO2:
not known

Gearbox:
6-speed manual or automatic

Drive:
rear wheels

Main body:
carbon fibre

Frame:
magnesium/aluminium/steel

Braking:
not known

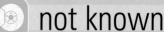

This book features some of the fastest, newest, and most technologically advanced supercars ever made in the USA. But lots of other supercars have been manufactured there. Here are a few of them:

MANUFACTURER: ACURA
MODEL: NSX
YEAR: 2016/17

Yes, Acura is owned by Honda. And yes, Honda is a Japanese company. But the Acura is proudly designed by Michelle Christensen (an American) and built in Marysville, Ohio (in the USA). A petrol-electric hybrid along the lines of a McLaren P1, the NSX reaches 100 kph in 3 seconds and has a top speed of over 300 kph.

MANUFACTURER: ALESSI
MODEL: AR-1
YEAR: 1979/2013

Alessi is a fibreglass manufacturer that, in 1979, decided to show off its skills by making a car with a fibreglass body. In 2013, the company released an updated version with a supercharged 6.2 litre V8 engine, able to reach 100 kph in about 3.5 seconds.

MANUFACTURER: DEVON
MODEL: GTX
YEAR: 2009

Looking like what would happen if an Alfa 8C had a baby with a Dodge Viper, the GTX is the supercar that never was (apart from two prototypes). It was actually based on a Dodge Viper, with carbon bodywork and an 8.4 litre V10 engine. When Dodge temporarily stopped making the Viper in 2010, the Devon disappeared.

MANUFACTURER: FORD
MODEL: GT
YEAR: 2005

Ford's first go at bringing back the spirit of its famous GT40. This car looks much more like the original than the 2016 GT. It was fast, too (0–100 kph in about 3.5 seconds) but when a car is this beautiful, that hardly matters.

MANUFACTURER: MOSLER
MODEL: MT900S
YEAR: 2003

With a 325 kW V8 engine and a weight of under 1,000 kg, this was a bit of a rocket ship. It was able to reach 100 kph in just over 3 seconds, and had a top speed of 288 kph. Mosler made the last ones in 2011, and went out of business in 2013.

MANUFACTURER: SALEEN
MODEL: S7 TWIN TURBO
YEAR: 2005

With a steel/aluminium frame and a carbon-fibre body, the Saleen was cutting-edge technology in 2000, when it first appeared. Weighing just about 1,300 kg and with a 7 litre twin-turbo V8 engine, it could hit 100 kph in under 3 seconds.

MANUFACTURER: TRION
MODEL: NEMESIS RR
YEAR: 2017?

Scheduled for construction in 2016 and sales in the first half of 2017, the Nemesis will be powered by a twin-turbo, 9-litre V8 engine. It will have almost 1,500 kW of power and be able to hit a top speed of over 430 kph.

American car companies have been making powerful cars for many years. In fact, in the 1930s Deusenberg made some of the world's most powerful cars. During the 1960s, in particular, several designs appeared that are still favourites today.

MANUFACTURER: PLYMOUTH
MODEL: ROADRUNNER SUPERBIRD
YEAR: 1970

The Superbird was an extra-long car with a crazy-looking, beaky nose and a rear wing so tall it looked like you could do pull-ups on it. They were fine on a race track, but so weird-looking that hardly anyone bought one. These days Superbirds are rare and valuable, and can sell for over £280,000.

MANUFACTURER: DEUSENBERG
MODEL: MODEL SSJ
YEAR: 1935

Just two of these were made – one for Gary Cooper, the other for Clark Gable. It looks like the kind of car an aristocrat is driven around in, but the SSJ's engine made 400 bhp – which is the same as a Ferrari 360 Modena.

MANUFACTURER: FORD
MODEL: MUSTANG GT289
YEAR: 1965

The first Ford Mustang had an engine that powered it to 100 kph in just over 5 seconds. If you got yours breathed on by a tuner (such as Carroll Shelby), the performance could be boosted by up to 30 per cent.

MANUFACTURER: SHELBY
MODEL: AC COBRA 260
YEAR: 1963

The Cobras started life in England, where AC built them without engines or gearboxes and sent them to Carroll Shelby, in the USA. There he fitted them with 4.2 litre V8 engines (instead of the 2.6 litre AC used). Racing Cobras went on to dominate the race scene in the USA.

MANUFACTURER: VECTOR
MODEL: W8 TWIN TURBO
YEAR: 1990

It looked like something styled by the designers of the original Battlestar Galactica, but the W8 had a lightweight aluminium frame and mostly carbon-fibre body. It could hit 100 kph in under 4 seconds.

PLACES TO VISIT

UK

NATIONAL MOTOR MUSEUM

Beaulieu
Brockenhurst
Hampshire
SO42 7ZN

http://nationalmotormuseum.org.uk/
Supercars
and
www.beaulieu.co.uk
Not a specialist supercar museum, and focusing mainly on British cars, the National Motor Museum is still a great place for car fans to visit. Its website has details of special displays, which sometimes include supercars.

BRITISH MOTOR MUSEUM

Banbury Road
Gaydon
Warwickshire
CV35 0BJ

www.britishmotormuseum.co.uk
Like the National Motor Museum, many of the cars are British, but other countries' cars are also on display.

HAYNES MOTOR MUSEUM

Haynes International Motor Museum
Sparkford
Yeovil
Somerset
BA22 7LH

www.haynesmotormuseum.com
With one of its collections called as 'Supercar Century', this fabulous museum is a must-visit if you are nearby.

USA

PETERSEN AUTOMOTIVE MUSEUM

6060 Wilshire Boulevard
Los Angeles, CA 90036

www.petersen.org
Filling an entire block of Los Angeles' Museum Row, the Petersen shows off all kinds of cars including supercars such as a 2006 Ford GT, a 1974 Ford Mustang and a 1933 Deusenberg SJ. But the most amazing car here is arguably a 1937 Delage D8-120S, an aluminium-only beauty that cost its original owner the equivalent of $1.79 million.

MULLIN AUTOMOBILE MUSEUM

1421 Emerson Ave
Oxnard CA 93033

www.mullinautomotivemuseum.
com

By no stretch a supercar museum, the Mullin is still worth a visit for any petrolhead or lover of beautiful car design. Specialising in classic cars, the museum has vehicles it's almost impossible to see anywhere else in the world.

SIMONE MUSEUM

6825 Norwitch Drive
Philadelphia, PA 19153

www.simeonemuseum.org
The Simone contains historic and modern race cars from all around the world, including a 1956 Mercedes SL300 Gullwing, 1966 Stingray 427 Roadster, 1958 Aston Martin DBR1, and a 1964 Shelby Cobra Daytona Coupé.

bhp short for brake horsepower, an alternative unit of power to kW

chassis the basic frame around which the rest of a car is built

concave curving inward

coupé car with a fixed, solid roof, two doors, and a sloping rear

downforce downward pressure on the tyres, which makes them grip the road better

exhaust headers metal pipes that join the exhaust pipes to the engine

front-mid engine positioned in the middle of the car, behind the front wheels

HANS short for Head And Neck Support, a special type of safety harness for motor racing; HANS harnesses help prevent head and neck injuries

HEMI special V6 and V8 engines built by Chrysler; the engines got their name because they originally had hemispherical cylinder heads (covers)

hybrid a type of engine that uses power from more than one source, usually in cars an internal combustion engine combined with electric motors

Indianapolis 500 famous US race over 200 laps of the Indianapolis Motor Speedway – which is 500 miles (805 km) in total

Kevlar® extremely strong artificial fibre, which can be mixed with other materials (such as carbon fibre or rubber) to make them stronger

kit car car that is delivered part-built, with the owner finishing the construction

limited restricted to a maximum speed

manual gears the driver has to change using a gearstick

muscle car a large, 2-door, high performance car with a powerful engine

petrolhead person who loves cars, especially high-performance cars

production car car that is built according to the same basic design for all customers

ride height the distance above the ground of a car's underside

splitter aerodynamic design that channels air through and around the car as it moves forward

spoiler wing at the back of a car that presses downward as air flows over it, improving the tyres' grip

supercharge feed extra air into an engine, which increases its power. A supercharger has the same effect as a turbocharger, but is powered in a different way

tune improve by making adjustments or changes

V8 engines are usually described using acombination of letters and numbers. A V8,for example, has 8 cylinders. They are arranged in two rows, joined at the bottom so that they make a V shape when seen from in front